WITHDRAWN

D0985089

Frank Peerman is president of the Peerman Corporation, Corpus Christi, Texas. He has a wide range of interests — his church, First Baptist of Corpus Christi, where he is a deacon and teacher; lay renewal, where he has close friends like Keith Miller, Howard Butt, and "Frog" Sullivan; his community, where he works with service boards and where he has been president of civic clubs; his home, where he and his wife, Betty Lee (Betsy), live; his hobbies — model trains, fishing, and writing; and children with whom he has worked in children's and youth baseball programs.

He is a graduate of Rice University. Frank and Betsy have three children, Patti, Nancy, and Terry. **See You in the Morning** centers around the death of Jody, the Peerman's youngest son.

SEE YOU IN THE MORNING

242.4
Pee

FRANK PEERMAN

SEE YOU IN THE MORNING

4890

BROADMAN PRESS
NASHVILLE, TENNESSEE

WOODMONT BAPTIST CHURCH LIBRARY
NASHVILLE, TENNESSEE

© Copyright 1976 ● BROADMAN PRESS
All rights reserved
4252-37
ISBN: 0-8054-5237-0

Subject headings: CONSOLATION // DEATH
Dewey Decimal Classification: 242.4
Library of Congress Catalog Card Number: 76-5296
Printed in the United States of America

DEDICATION
To My Beloved Son

JODY SECOR PEERMAN
June 5, 1957—September 1, 1972

ACKNOWLEDGMENTS

To Betsy, Patti, Nancy, and Terry: my deep love and appreciation. They walked the same path with me and shared my heartaches and victories.

To my friend, Keith Miller: my love and gratitude. Without his encouragement, counsel, and technical advice, the manuscript would not have been written.

To the many others who shared my loss: my love always.

FRANK PEERMAN

FOREWORD

Bewildered Christians who have looked up at a cold, starry night through tears of grief and screamed "Why?" will find an understanding friend and guide in Frank Peerman and SEE YOU IN THE MORNING.

This is not a book of preaching, but rather a Christian's pilgrimage which hundreds of stunned silent pilgrims are beginning, even as you are reading these words.

The Frank Peerman who wrote this book is a different man from the successful, moral, respectable, converted deacon I met almost fifteen years ago. Through his own wrestling with the angel of death, which visited his home, have been distilled some simple yet profound discoveries about the risk of opening your heart enough to let other people in—and the fact that pain may come into us through the same door—but also a measure of the fullness of life. Here, those of you who have known grief will recognize the stages of disbelief, frustration, anger, despair, and finally a "wisdom of the bloodstream" too deep for words, which tells us that tragedy can have a *meaning* in our lives, even if we can only stand dumb before the question "why"? Watching Frank balk at the pain and then learn to live with it, one discovers again the strange truth of the gospel of Jesus Christ—that in some mysterious way pain and perhaps grief are prerequisites for the kind of love and compassion which can enter other people's suffering with them and walk through it.

Having watched some of this story being lived out in the author's life, I have seen that out of the ashes of a sincere conventional Christian faith and respectable success, God can raise something very special: a sensitive, loving, human being.

I recommend this book to you who may be walking alone or with a friend or family member through the hell of grief. For beyond the agony Frank Peerman has found hope.

KEITH MILLER
Port Aransas, Texas

CONTENTS

INTRODUCTION

The grass is beginning to carpet his grave now, and the shock of his sudden death no longer rolls over me in such pounding waves. Time is slowly dimming the memories, and his footsteps in the sands of life are gradually fading away.

He was all a father could hope for in a son. He filled my heart with love and my ego with pride; excelling in school, athletics, music, and most of the ways we value excellence. Everything was going for him but time.

What a kind, gentle lad he was. For him, life was never dull. He was all boy, with an insatiable zest for living, a warm sense of humor, and a simple faith in the goodness of mankind.

His life in this world ended in the blinding lights of an onrushing car, the sudden screaming of tires on a city street, and the deathly silence that follows the thousands of such tragic accidents that happen each year. The police hold his crumpled bicycle as evidence in the forthcoming trial. He had lived fifteen years, two months, and twenty-seven days.

For me, the relentless, daily tragedies of life were no longer cold, impersonal statistics that happen to someone else. With his death, I joined the legions of parents, wives, and children whose loved ones have been killed in senseless wars; of stunned souls who sat in lonely hospital rooms, as doctors gently shook their heads; of shocked survivors who listened in disbelief to messages of sudden, accidental, death; of those who watched dear ones suddenly slump forward in agony or quietly slip away in the night; of lonely, miserable, grief-stricken humanity everywhere.

To these lonely souls, and those destined to join them in the days ahead, this book is written. It is the testimony of one man who lost his son and, through his ensuing grief, rediscovered his Father's love. It is not a textbook on grief. I'm not qualified for such an undertaking, nor is that my purpose. I simply want to share my experiences with others, in the hope that, in their "moment of truth," they will remember one who traveled that same painful road.

The early drafts of this manuscript are sprinkled with tears—tears of pity and loneliness and despair and thankfulness. It has not been easy to expose so much of my secret self, and yet, the writing of it has been therapeutic in many ways.

Some of you may question my conversations with God and Satan; there was a time in my life when I would have.

The conversations are real to me, however, even as God and Satan are now, also, very real. I do not claim to hear their spoken words, but their presence, thoughts, messages, and interventions are a daily part of my life.

I have tried to write with honesty and truth as best I understand it. Please read with your heart. For within our hearts we often see more truth than our minds will ever perceive.

Love is the beautiful and ultimate fulfillment of life. And yet, each time we give a part of ourselves to another, we expose our hearts to pain. For sooner or later, grief seems to come to most of us who have loved.

Hopefully, by sharing our pain and anguish and ultimate discovery or rediscovery of Christ, we may be able to lessen the fears that grip us all, and allow God's love to brighten and enrich our days.

FRANK PEERMAN
Corpus Christi, Texas

WOODMONT BAPTIST CHURCH LIBRARY
NASHVILLE, TENNESSEE

1.
FEAR

Beneath tangled, bushy brows, the preacher's eyes bored into the hot, musky air of the revival tent. His gaunt frame seemed to tower above everyone—the worn, black, ill-fitting coat sagging on his bony shoulders. In his left hand, he held a tattered Bible pressed against his breast as though to shield himself from the forces of evil.

Like an instrument of God's judgment, his right arm swung back and forth above the people; the long, crooked forefinger pausing first upon one—then another—accusing, condemning, striking fear into the hearts of all but the self-righteous.

Words spewed from his mouth and fell, like scalding fire, upon the huddled souls; words like: "wicked, sinful, evil, vile," and names like: "Lord God, God Almighty, Jesus Christ, and the Evil One." But the thing that struck me with more force than all else was when he screamed out, "Thou shalt *fear* the Lord thy God!" or something like that.

Every nerve in my young body was trembling. I slumped down on the wooden bench, and hid my face in the folds of mother's skirt, expecting to be struck dead at any moment.

As the preacher's voice rolled on, I heard moans from some of the people, while others were shouting, "Amen!"

I cautiously lifted my head, and glanced fearfully around the tent. . . .

The bodies of the mourners began to twist and writhe in spastic movements. The preacher walked out among them; stopping at different ones, and placing his hand upon their heads; all the while exhorting them, "Confess your sins." "Beg God for mercy." And then he raised his hand toward heaven and prayed for God to save them from hell.

There were some who began crying and shouting, "Praise the Lord!" and "Hallelujah!" The sounds seemed to reverberate within the tent, to mingle with the flat, tiny notes of an ancient piano, the anguished cries of the sinners, and the exultations of the godly.

The dust rose from the dirt floor, and formed halos, of swarming bugs around bare light bulbs hanging from the tent poles. Fantastic shadows on the tent sides seemed to ring the scene with demonic forms, leaping about in the outer darkness and threatening to break through the thin canvas, to devour, destroy, and worst of all, to carry off into the inky blackness of the night.

Such are the recollections I have, as a young boy, of traveling revival meetings held in our neighborhood. The year was around 1927, in the growing city of Houston, Texas, an overgrown town nestled on the banks of Buffalo Bayou, where horse-drawn wagons delivered blocks of melting ice, and boys wore Bobby Jones style knickers and caps.

Though the scene seems as vivid to me as if it happened yesterday, you must remember I was very young and not entirely reliable as a witness. The episode almost *scared me to death*, and played a large part in creating the anxieties that plagued me for years.

Fear became a controlling force in my life—the kind of fear that creates in one the terrible dread of danger, pain, or disaster. When the Bible said, "Fear the Lord," I did not understand it to mean extreme reverence of God. I thought it meant what I read it to say: "Be good, or woe unto you, for God has no mercy on sinners."

I obeyed my parents, or they "wore me out" with a doubled belt. I obeyed the law, because my dad threatened to send me to the bad-boys home, if I didn't. I could hardly sneeze without breaking one of God's laws; which meant that, at any moment, I could be *struck dead.* I really tried to obey God, because *death* was my greatest fear.

Death was not waking up each morning, no more tomorrows, or dreams, or fun, or laughter, or play. Death was a hole in the ground and darkness and never, never, never, never. But thank goodness, death was a long way off, and only came to very old people.

I hated fear, or what it did to me.

Once, after dark, my dad hid under a bridge behind our house, and when I crossed, he leaped out, screaming like a wild banshee. He meant it as a practical joke, but my sense of humor had not quite developed that far. Wild with fright, my only reaction was to run—and run I did. I ran and ran and ran, unable to stop myself. I knew who had scared me. I also knew no one was chasing me. But facts had no control over my legs. They drove me on until, exhausted, I stumbled and fell beside the road, sobbing with self-hatred and shame.

Having no concept of the psychology of human anxieties, I decided that I had to face those things I feared; even if it meant being eaten alive by demons, or tortured, or even struck dead by God. Dying once *couldn't* be worse than being afraid to die every day of my life.

So, I resolved to make myself face those things that frightened me. The opportunity to put my new resolve into practice came sooner than I expected.

Riding my bicycle to school the next day, I spied a group of "tough guys" on the path ahead of me. My instinct was to ride around them and avoid their taunts. Instead, I continued toward them. As I approached, one of them stuck a stick into the spokes of my bicycle, and I went sailing, head over heels, into the dirt. They roared with laughter.

I picked myself up, walked over to the guy, and asked why he did that. And before he could reply, I hit him in the mouth. The only trouble was, I didn't hit him hard enough, because, in the ensuing fight, he nearly killed me! But, to my amazement, I discovered that the lumps and bruises didn't hurt nearly as much as I feared, and the self-respect I gained for myself was worth ten times the pain of my wounds.

In the days to come, I discovered other ways to test my newfound courage. I walked alone at night through the streets and ravines of the bayous near my home. At first, every step was a nightmare of terror, but no monsters devoured me, and I began to recognize reality in the foreboding shapes that once seemed so grotesque and frightening to me.

I flaunted every superstition I had been warned against: walked under ladders, swept trash out the back door after dark, put hats on my bed, broke mirrors, opened umbrellas inside the house, let black cats cross my path. I dared them all, but no calamity befell me. Whatever I feared, I tried to face—except for God. Somehow I could never bring myself to tempt God, even though I feared him above all else.

I had challenged many of my fears and survived, but it was to be a while before my first *real* confrontation with God. The incident happened in the First Christian Church in Houston. It was mother's church, and we generally went there on Sundays. My dad had been christened in the Episcopal Church, and his name was engraved on a bronze plaque as one of the boys who had gone off to the "war to end all wars."

One Sunday, the pastor said something that caught my attention. I put aside the picture I was drawing, and listened to what he was saying. In my young mind, this was the story I heard:

An angel from heaven told the shepherds and Wise Men that a baby named Jesus was born in a manger. Jesus was the Son of God, and when he grew up, he spent all his time healing the sick and blind and crippled, and telling them about God. He told them God loved them and didn't want them to go to hell for their sins.

Jesus loved the people so much that he gave his life to pay for their sins. All you had to do to be saved was believe in him and accept him as your Lord and Savior.

And then the pastor told how Jesus let them nail his hands and feet to a wooden cross, and how he prayed for the people, even as he was dying.

But Jesus did not stay dead. Three days later, on the day we call Easter, God raised him from the dead. Jesus overcame death, just as he promised, for himself and for all who believe in him.

As the pastor talked, I seemed to hear Jesus talking to me—telling me that he loved me and, if I loved him and trusted him, I could overcome the greatest fear of all—death!

My fear of God was like most of my other fears—

imaginary. But Jesus loved me and would someday stand beside me when I went to heaven and met God. And death would be nothing more than falling asleep and waking up in a place where I would never have to be afraid again. On that day, even though I was still a young boy, I placed my life in Christ's care.

Because of all the frightening recollections those early anxieties etched so deeply in my mind, I would not be honest if I said that, since that time, I have never been afraid. I still have my moments. But, long ago, I ceased to cower before fear.

Later in life, I found myself transferring some of my old childhood fears of death to fears for my children's safety. I sometimes wondered how I would react if anything ever happened to one of them.

This is the story of that day—*the day death came.*

2.
THE
NIGHTMARE

It was a day like any other; a pleasant Friday evening with expectations of a fun-filled Labor Day weekend ahead. We had just finished watching the Olympic Games on television, and while my wife, Betsy, went into the rear of the house, I remained to hear the evening news.

The 10:00 P.M. newscast began with a flash announcement: Two youths on bicycles had been struck by an auto. One was dead, the other critically injured. No further details were available.

I heard it in the back of my mind—another tragedy. "There are so many these days," I thought. For some reason, the word *youths* meant two boys, and Jody, our youngest, had gone to visit his girlfriend, Ivy Hagens. Because it did not concern me, I brushed it from my mind.

As the newscast continued, Betsy came into the room and asked if I had heard the announcement. She was never completely at ease whenever any of our children were out after dark. She reminded me that Jody was always home by 10:15 and wondered if I were concerned. I said, "No, Honey, don't worry, it was two boys. Jody's at Ivy's house." Her mention of the time, however, made me realize that Jody *was* late, and that was so unlike him.

And then I recognized what she was saying. It *could* be Jody. Tiny alarms went off, and a nagging anxiety began to creep into my mind. We sat there, each trying not to let the other know of our rising fears. It was the horrible uncertainty that gnawed at us; the fear began to slowly inch up through our bodies with a suffocating persistency. I got up and began to pace the room. When I could stand it no longer, I called Ivy's home.

Mr. Hagens answered, and I asked if Jody were there. He said, "Yes, he and Ivy are on the front porch." I hesitated—"Thank God!" Then, with what I hoped was a reassuring laugh, I told him about the news report and added, "I'm just being an overly concerned father; I knew everything was all right. But, would you mind calling him to the phone?" Somehow I had to hear Jody's voice. This thing had gone too far, and I needed more than secondhand assurances.

When he returned to the phone, he said, "Mr. Peerman, they're not on the porch. But they can't be very far away. They were there a few minutes ago. When did the accident happen?" My heart sank. I said, "The report indicated it happened about 8:45 P.M." He seemed relieved, because he was almost positive they could not have been gone more than fifteen minutes. We tried to reassure each other and rang off.

Neither Betsy nor I were reassured. In fact, we were becoming more frightened by the moment, and yet, we were afraid to call the authorities. While the uncertainty was terrible, the fear of what we might learn was even worse. If it were Jody and Ivy, which one was dead? Oh, God! What a horrible thought!

The telephone rang with a nerve-shattering sound and I answered, almost too scared to speak. It was Mr. Hagens. He said that they, too, were concerned, and suggested that we call the authorities. We agreed that he would call the hospital, and I, the police.

Dialing that number was one of the hardest things I have ever done in my life. I was connected with the dispatcher; took a deep breath, and asked if they had identified the victims of the bicycle-auto accident.

He said, "The girl is critically injured, and we have identified her, but not the boy."

The girl! Oh, no! When I heard that one was a *girl*, I could barely speak. In a choked voice, I asked if her name were Hagens and again held my breath.

After a pause, he said, "We cannot give out any information until her family has been notified."

I almost screamed out to him, "I *have* to know. My son and a girl are out riding their bicycles together. You can at least tell me if the girl's name is Hagens!"

The officer hesitated and then said, "No, Mr. Peerman, her name is not Hagens—it's a Spanish surname."

"Thank God!" I cried and hung up the phone. Every nerve in my body was jerking in spastic trembles. I told Betsy what he said. We looked at each other, and somehow we *knew* the information was wrong.

To this day, I don't know how we knew. But we did. Later we discovered that the police had recorded the wrong license number from Ivy's crumpled bicycle.

I tried to call the Hagens, but their line was busy. I tried again and again to no avail. Unable to stand the suspense, I told Betsy I had to go to their house—I had to *know!* Nothing, short of seeing Jody with my own eyes and holding him in my arms would do now.

The drive was a nightmare. I followed the route I thought Jody might be taking on his way home. At each intersection, I looked in all directions, frantically searching for him, my eyes boring into the darkness for a glimpse of that familiar figure. The streets were vacant, and the closer I came to Ivy's house, the more my desperate hope faded.

I began to plead aloud to God, begging him: "Oh, please God. Let Jody be there. Please God! Please! Please. . . ."

As I approached the front of the Hagen house, a car was backing out of the drive. I quickly got out. The rear door of the other car opened, and Ivy, the girl with whom Jody had been riding, came toward me. Tears were streaming down her face.

I was bewildered! How could Ivy be all right? Where was Jody? Was he in the car? Why the tears? Was it because they had frightened us so? Oh, Lord, what was happening?

And suddenly I recognized the horrible, unbelievable truth. *It wasn't Ivy at all!* It was her older sister, *Dawn!*

Jody was dead! Ivy was critically injured! And in that instant, a part of me also died. . . .

The human brain is a remarkable mechanism; when it receives information that threatens its survival, sometimes it simply rejects it. In the shock of that awful moment, I can only recall one reaction: I began to run in crazy circles, screaming aloud, "No! No! No! No! Oh, no God— not Jody!"

Dawn was wringing her hands, and asking me, over and over, "Mr. Peerman, are you all right?"

What a horrible experience it must have been for her. Having just found out the tragic news about Ivy, she and her family were rushing to the hospital, when I suddenly appeared. She wasn't even aware that I didn't know. Oh, Lord! Life can be so cruel sometimes.

I couldn't answer Dawn. My shocked subconscious took over, and I stumbled to the car, knowing that I had to get to Betsy; to tell her, to hold her, to hold on to her.

In that wild drive home, I passed the elementary and

junior high schools Jody had attended. Thousands of images of him flashed before my eyes: from a small boy, through gangling youth, to young manhood. I passed the practice fields where we had spent so many happy afternoons in Little League and Pony League baseball. I passed the corner where, following baseball or football or basketball practice each day, he would grab the wheel of the car and say, "Icee, got'ta have an Icee." And, after making some comment about it being too near dinner time, I'd generally give in and head for the store.

Looking back, that trip seems like a lifetime. The futile, hoping, searching, pleading of the drive over; the unbearable shock of learning the truth; and the unbelievable despair of the drive back.

I turned into the driveway of our home and, through the window, could see Betsy hanging up the phone; it was obvious that she, too, knew the truth. I rushed to her, crying out, "Honey, it was Jody! It was Jody!" As we clung pathetically and helplessly to each other, I shall never forget her words, spoken between wracking sobs, "Our lives will never again be the same." And I knew it was so.

The nightmare had become reality. Death, the terrible enemy I had feared so long, had passed over me, and claimed the sweet, young life of my precious son. God, what irony!

I KNOW, NOW, WHY

I know not how a hummingbird sounds,
    Nor have heard an angel sigh;
But a broken heart, like a crippled bird,
    Cries mournfully to the sky.
And I know, now, why some seek to die.
    I know, now, why.

3.
A
NIGHT
IN HELL

I had often wondered whether hell were a state of mind rather than a place. The mental anguish and torture I endured on the night Jody was killed could not have been anything but hell. There may be degrees of hell, and I'll not split hairs with anyone as to who has experienced the worst. But I'm not like Job in the Bible. That single experience was enough to last me a lifetime.

The preceding nightmare was a horrible dream. But in that dream there was hope, and I held tenaciously to the promise of awakening, and the blessed relief that would follow. When the final hope was gone, the door to the dungeon of reality slammed closed, and the trap of hell was sprung.

Like a caged animal, my mind struck out in all directions, tearing at the bars and hurling itself against the walls. But the walls resisted the bull-like charges and only increased the agony. And then, with human cunning, my mind resorted to reason, and began to systematically search for a hidden opening, a crevice, a crack—anything! There were none; only endless blind alleys and hopeless frustration.

I cried out to Betsy, but she was imprisoned in her own hell, and I could not reach her—nor she me. We seemed to be miles apart, almost in different worlds, alone with our own private thoughts and broken dreams.

I paced the floor restlessly, wanting to go somewhere, to be with someone, but I didn't know where or with whom. I walked out into the night, stumbling blindly over obstacles, mumbling incoherent, wild thoughts, wanting to cry or to die. And then, I realized what my subconscious mind was seeking:

I was looking for someone to *tell me it wasn't so!* No wonder I could not make any sense out of my actions. It seems to me there's a thin line, sometimes, between sanity and insanity.

In trance-like automation, I remembered the responsibilities of life and began to look around me. Our daughters, Patti and Nancy, had heard the tragic news and, though brokenhearted, were bravely trying to help us. Someone had to call Terry, our older son. He was a student at Baylor University in Waco. He happened to be visiting his girl friend, Mary Anderson, at Texas Christian University in Fort Worth. We left word, and he called around midnight. When told the tragic news, he expressed all our feelings with his heartbreaking question, "Why did it have to be Jody? The world needs more people like him."

Gradually the entire family and closest friends, from Ohio to California, were notified, and they began making plans to be with us. The thought of Terry driving 400 miles from Fort Worth, in his emotionally shattered state of mind, terrified me. I had lost one son. . . .

We could not get immediate reservations on a commercial airline, so I turned to a dear friend, Ralph Storm, who had a private airplane. When I told him my problem, his only words were, "Give me Terry's telephone number, I'll have my pilot meet me at the plane; I want two pilots for this flight." He had Terry at our door before daylight the following morning. Such was the caliber of our friends. How can one ever repay such favors?

It was necessary for Betsy and me to go to the hospital. My brother, Bob, and his wife, Nancy, took us. At the emergency room, we met Ivy's parents. Ivy was still alive but in critical condition. I prayed that God would spare her; one young life from such a tragedy was enough! It was not to be, however, for within a couple of days, Ivy joined Jody. How I have grieved for the agony the Hagens family must have endured while Ivy lingered those two days.

Ivy was like a breath of spring. Her youthful beauty and sparkling vitality made each moment with her a happy experience. We had not known her long. Jody met her in a speech class they shared at school. She must have had the same effect on him, for it seemed to us that, one day, like most adolescent boys, he was wondering what anyone ever saw in *girls;* and the next thing we knew, he was spending every available moment in his room talking to her on the telephone. There wasn't much conversation, but I am not so old I cannot remember the magic that occurs when a special girl is on the other end of that long, thin wire. For Jody, Ivy was the wonder, the excitement, and the magic of first love. Somehow, it's a good feeling to know that he went home to God riding by her side.

While we were in the hospital, Bob performed the gruesome task of identifying Jody's body. I didn't know he had handled that chore until weeks later, when I saw the death certificate. I knew something had shaken him to the core of his being, but I didn't realize what it was. I could never have done it—never!

My heart was broken, my world shattered, and my hope

gone; there was no rationality to my thoughts. It was a time to cry. I have come to deeply resent the stupid notion that it is unmanly to cry. Such an insidious untruth could only have come from Satan's genius. Through the generations, this false manly pride had been so deeply bred into me that, though my heart was broken, I could not shed a single tear. I resorted instead to rage—a towering, righteous, inarticulate, violent, impotent rage! I wanted to destroy everything in my sight. Oh, God, how I hated death!

When we returned home, I stepped out of the car and the first thing I saw was the basketball hoop on the garage roof. Below the hoop, I could see that tall young figure with raven black hair, leaping and twisting with the beautiful coordination of a natural athlete. I had a wild desire to leap toward the hoop myself. To grab it, to tear it loose from its mountings, and to crush it into bits. I hated anything that reminded me of him. At the same time, I wanted to hold it close to me because it was a part of him, and so I loved it.

Several close friends were waiting in our home, among them, Vernon Elmore, our beloved pastor. Later, as we walked alone in the front yard, I poured out my rage to him. I thought of the impending funeral service and told him of my hatred for funerals with their fancy customs and feeble words, all of which meant nothing and only prolonged the agony. I told him how much I loved and respected him, but added, "What do you really know about Jody, or my relationship with him, or how deeply I loved him? What words can you say? I'll tell you what—nothing! I don't want a funeral. Why can't they cremate his body and throw the ashes away? He lives there no longer—he's with God. Why must we suffer through such an ordeal?"

He listened patiently to my tirade, and being the gentle, understanding man he is, put his arm around my shoulders, and I knew he understood and loved me. I also knew that Jody's funeral service would be in good hands—and it was.

From childhood, certain aspects of death and funerals have held an eerie horror for me. Perhaps it was caused by an incident that happened at my grandfather's funeral: Someone took me to the casket and said, "Kiss Grandpa good-bye, honey." I shall never forget those words, or the shock that followed. In my child's mind, I knew, even then, that the cold, made-up face was not my grandfather. Grandpa was gone; I didn't know where, but I knew he wasn't in that fancy, satin-lined box, and I wanted no part of it. Since that day, I have no other recollection of him, no mental picture of him at all, save that waxen face on a satin pillow.

As I grew older, I seldom went to funerals. But that was selfish of me, and I found I could not avoid them. In this case, however, I could not risk the danger of looking at my son's lifeless body. I wanted to remember him as I had known him in life.

I accept my own death now as a very real part of life, and no longer have an unusual fear of it. It is but the next step in my Christian journey. I don't look forward to it because I love life, and death is an unknown; but I trust God even though I fear, to some degree, that which I don't understand. It is the death of my loved ones that I fear; I know, now, what pain it can bring.

I don't believe that we are only these *bodies* in which we dwell. I believe that we are, also, *spirits*, made in the likeness of God's Spirit; and in some miraculous way, we will someday transcend the boundaries of space and time, into a new life with our Creator, the likeness of which my mind, in its wildest imagination, cannot even begin to conceive.

But while we Christians may look forward to paradise, I don't know too many who are in such a great hurry to get there—at least I'm not. I find life exciting and precious, and resent the loss of any portion of its full allotment.

Such were my feelings about Jody. He was cheated out of so much, and I resented it! That may seem to be a contradiction, but that's how I am. Call it illogical or human—it's probably both—but when death comes to someone so young, resentment can be as natural as breathing.

I did not want to sleep that night; I was afraid of the dreams, and the waking up.

And I could not pray. My resentment and furious anger were too strong. I was angry with God for not protecting my son; it would have been such a little thing for him. I resented life, with its tragic, senseless accidents. I blamed myself, because, somehow, I felt guilty; and above all else, I hated death.

Around 4:30 in the morning, I had a sudden, strong feeling of doubt—of uncertainty. Like one in a dream, I walked toward Jody's room and opened the door. How many nights I had done that when he was a child, had looked in to see his tousled head on the rumpled pillow, had leaned over to gently brush his cheek. . . .

I stared at the smooth, unrumpled bedspread—barren and empty and cold—and all the doubts drained away; I knew he would never come home again.

4.
A
STORY

Grief, despair, and loneliness had reduced me to such a miserable state, I wished I could run far away from it all.

I remembered an incident that happened in our neighborhood several months before. Maybe if I tell you the story now, it will help you to understand.

The aviary nestled on an island in the center of a small lake. Inside the enclosure, wild doves flew among flowering trees. The sounds of falling water could be heard as it tumbled over a rock fall and into a shallow pond. White ducks swam lazily on the surrounding lake, trailing V-shaped wakes that crossed and recrossed on the mirror surface of the water.

Overhead, in the bright sky, two white pigeons flew, side by side, with effortless grace and beauty. For several minutes, they circled the island, and then, dived slowly down, fluttering around the wire enclosure, before landing on a low stone wall. In the bobbing, cooing way of pigeons, they paced back and forth on the wall, heads tilting from side to side, as if trying to understand the wire and the strange birds that made sounds similar to their own.

It was a pleasant, peaceful place and food was available in the area where the ducks were fed daily. People came regularly, and they were kind, and the pigeons accepted them. The female had less fear and took bread from the people's hands, while the male seemed to hold back in a somewhat disapproving and cautious way. Later when they perched on top of the aviary, it seemed to me that the male tried to warn her about such carelessness, but she was young and didn't know fear.

What a beautiful thing the female was, with soft feathers as white as fresh-fallen snow. Her dainty head and body seemed to move with a grace that was pure delight to the eye. And her eyes! They were as gentle as moonglow, and completely captivated the male with their loveliness. To say he loved her was totally inadequate. He seemed to adore her.

As the days went by, the people became increasingly fond of the white pigeons and began to think of them as their own. (It seems to be a way of people to want to own things of beauty.) Coupled with owning was the fear of losing. "What if they should fly away, or be killed?" they asked. "We should catch them and put them in the aviary."

Catching the female was easy; she trusted them completely, and came willingly toward their outstretched hands. When they suddenly grabbed her, she seemed to cry out in fear and began to struggle, trying desperately to free herself. Wild with fright, her mate flew into the air, and circled frantically above the scene—helpless and terrified.

They gently placed the female in a cardboard box, and closed the top. In the dark confines, she thrashed wildly about until exhausted, then huddled in a corner, trembling and afraid.

The people wondered how they were going to catch her mate. He had always been more wary; he wouldn't come near them now. There was a smaller aviary on the island; it had been built for quail, but was empty at the present time. "Why not put the box, containing the female, inside?" they reasoned. "Leave the door open, and the male will join her." It seemed a simple solution.

They placed the box on the ground, propped the door open, and went away, confident that the male would join her, and they would have them both.

Shortly after they left, the male glided down to the roof of the aviary and called out to the female. She didn't answer. Frantically he called, again and again, but she was in shock and could not make a sound.

As darkness approached, he flew to the ground outside the wire, and strained to get a glimpse of her within the darkened interior. All he could see was the box. Back and forth he paced beside the wire. There was no opening, and he didn't know about the door on the other side.

As the light faded from the sky, the night became increasingly black. He was torn between his desire to be near her and his instinctive fear of the ground. Finally, his fear won out, and he flew back to the aviary roof.

But there was no peace, only nervous restlessness. He could not stop his ceaseless pacing along the roof edge, and his calls became so plaintive and sad. Into the night, he maintained his lonely vigil, feathers fluffed against the chill; his eyes and senses alert to danger.

Sometime after midnight, he sensed a movement among the bushes below, and froze! For what seemed like hours he held his body motionless, his eyes boring into the shadows of a bush. And then he saw the cat. . . .

It had begun to creep silently toward the aviary, its long tail twitching from side to side, its body moving in the low, stealthy crouch of the feline.

The pigeon leaped into the air, his wings beating frantically! He dived madly toward the cat, but he had no defense against the beast, and he knew it—and so did the cat.

As the pigeon flew wildly above, the cat ignored him, and began to slowly circle the walls of the aviary. He came to the open door and paused, testing the air, looking from side to side. He was not comfortable going into the enclosure, but his hunger was greater than his fear, and he went through the door. . . .

When the male pigeon heard the first tearing sounds of the cardboard box, his mind exploded, and he began to climb higher into the sky; higher, and higher, and higher he flew. The winds buffeted him, and he fought savagely to maintain his control. The swirling clouds alternately blanked out the lights of the city below; the whistling wind roared in his ears; his sense of location and direction was gone; he himself was gone—only his instincts remained. He seemed suspended in time.

Hours later, and bone-weary, he began to lose altitude. Toward dawn, he glided onto the cornice of a large building, and crept under an overhang. Physically and emotionally exhausted, he slept.

The morning sun awakened him, and, for a blessed moment, he remembered nothing. But like an onrushing torrent, the horrible events of the preceding night swirled upon him, and with them came the shame. He hated himself for flying away, for leaving her. It would have been better to have died. He had to return; there was no other way. He knew it, and lifted himself wearily into the morning sky.

The gardener arrived on the island, and began his morning chores. Over in the smaller aviary, something strange caught his eye, and he walked toward it. In stunned disbelief, he viewed the carnage: the shredded, overturned box; the feathers, scattered among the gravel, their brilliant whiteness stained with the crimson red blood.

He ran to tell the people, and they came in small groups. Some were quietly crying, some outrageously angry and seeking revenge, some shrugging their shoulders in resignation and muttering what a shame it was.

Someone thought of the male, and asked about him. Then they spied him, flying alone in the sky above the island. Silently, his wings pumped sluggishly in the morning air, and his body slowly descended, to land softly on the aviary roof.

He seemed free from any fear of the people. He was indifferent to them or to fear. It was more of a loneliness, a pathetic, aching misery—a deep yearning for things that once were, but could be no more.

The people spoke in low, hushed tones, trying to reconstruct what had happened. Some inquired about the cat, and wanted to kill it. "Why blame the cat?" another asked. "He was hungry and the pigeon offered food; it's his way of life. Perhaps we should blame ourselves."

Somehow, the pigeon seemed to understand their words, but understanding could not fill the void or the loneliness; what did understanding have to do with his loss? He turned away from the people, tucked his head beneath a wing, as though to shut out the world around him, and in that secret place in his heart, he cried.

The gardener began to clean the aviary, and the people slowly dispersed toward their surrounding homes.

Soon the island was quiet again, except for the sounds of life and the distant cry of a sea gull as he soared high overhead. Sensing the tragedy, the mourning doves perched quietly on the branches of a wild olive tree, their activities suspended. Almost imperceptible, a single dove began a soft, plaintive cooing. The others cautiously joined in as they shared the pigeon's grief.

I sat on the outer bank of the lake and grieved for the pigeon, but I knew I could not help him.

For several days, I watched him. At first he would not leave the aviary where she had been killed. He seemed to need nothing, or no one. He was in a state of shock, and nothing could reach him. One afternoon he glided over to the dove house, as if seeking fellowship. The doves were busily occupied with their own lives and ignored him, so he paced back and forth on the rock wall, cooing softly to himself.

He left the wall and flew to the ground outside the place where he had last seen her. It seemed to me that he was searching for her, and I understood, remembering that first morning when I had gone into Jody's room.

As I watched, he gazed toward the sky, as though listening to some far-off sound—a beckoning call. His head turned toward the empty aviary; he seemed torn and undecided. He wanted to stay, but the call was too strong.

Spreading his wings to catch the breeze, he lifted into the air and began climbing in ever-widening circles—his eyes fixed on the island. Suddenly, his wings tilted, and he slipped downward to make one last pass over the island. Then, once again, he leveled off and flew upward and away; his white body fading into nothingness against the endless sky. . . .

As I watched him vanish from sight, my soul reached out to him in a kinship of grief. I turned slowly and walked away, my mind returning to that first day following the death of my son.

5.
THE
FIRST
DAY

People began arriving early that morning. People who were more than acquaintances or friends or loved ones. They were God's angels; some bearing delicious food, some lovely flowers, and all of them bringing themselves to share our grief. There wasn't a single need they didn't fill with efficiency and grace and love. They will always occupy a special place in my heart.

My older brother, Wallace, drove in from Austin with his family. Oh, the happy, carefree days we had shared in the past. The memories rolled across the screen of my mind in an avalanche of sights and sounds. Where had those golden days gone? Days of bright sun on shimmering waters, of gnarled oaks and cool shade, of picnic baskets and hungry mouths, and happiness that sent the heart soaring among the white, fluffy clouds. Did the memories of such days dwell in their hearts as they did in mine?

My sister, Bernice and her family, flew in from Las Vegas and, as I held them in my arms, I'll never forget the tears that were in each of their eyes. Perhaps they were thinking back to a month before; the summer when Betsy and I took Jody and Bob's son, Greg, on a wonderful motorhome trip through the northeastern states and Canada.

Knowing that Jody was rapidly growing up, and would soon be beyond such vacations with mom and dad, we planned the trip especially for him. He wanted Greg to go because they were the closest of friends. They even planned to be business partners someday—like their dads.

The trip was pure pleasure. On the last leg, we swung south through Las Vegas, and spent a couple of days with Bernice and her family. We didn't get to see them often, and it was one of the highlights of our vacation.

But there were no highlights on that fateful Saturday. Gloom and misery hung over us like a pall. As I wandered among family and friends, grief seemed to close in on me—strangling me in its icy tentacles. I stumbled into the yard and slumped down at the base of a tree. No one followed. I don't know how long I sat there, my head on my knees, my eyes closed, lonely and miserable beyond words.

With a sigh of surrender, I murmured; "Oh, Lord, help me. . . ." In the silence that followed, I suddenly knew that the Holy Spirit was there. I seemed to hear him say, "I UNDERSTAND, MY SON. TRUST ME AND ALL WILL BE WELL. I WILL NOT LEAVE YOU."

I had known that feeling before, when the Holy Spirit was upon me; had sensed his presence, seemed to hear his words. It always happened in times of crisis or decisions, whenever I submitted my will to his. It was not new to me; but this time it was more vivid, and a great sigh escaped from my body as the tension began to dissolve. I grew limp and seemed to slip into unconsciousness, as in a dream. I wanted to speak, but no words came from my lips. I could have remained there forever, suspended in the peace of that moment.

As the moment began to fade, I raised my head, and realized for the first time since the tragedy that, with *his* love, I might be able to bear even this. I remembered his words, "BLESSED ARE THEY THAT MOURN, FOR THEY SHALL BE COMFORTED." I had never before understood those words, but suddenly they became clearer. God can comfort only those who *need* comforting. Christ knew the human agony brought on by death. He came to conquer it. In his presence I found a peace that was beyond understanding. It was miraculous how most of the pain and misery and loneliness seemed to go away.

Throughout the remainder of that day and evening, a steady procession of friends came to share our loss—our friends as well as Jody's and Ivy's. I remembered, with shame, the times in the past when I had failed to visit friends in grief, excusing my selfishness with the alibi that they needed to be alone, and there was nothing I could do. I found out I was wrong.

Words cannot express the strength we received from so many dear ones. Even though we had to bear our grief alone, it was somehow easier when shared. We were thankful to God for their presence and love. We were also grateful for their attempts to comfort us.

But Betsy and I really didn't want to be *comforted*. To be comforted is to be soothed or cheered; we didn't want that. *We wanted our son back!* When death came, one of the shocking discoveries to us was how *permanent* it was. We could not fix it or change it or do anything about it. We just had to accept it, and it hurt like hell itself! It seems to me that we can stand by friends and love them until their pain begins to subside, and they need this support and love. But true comfort comes only from God. At least, that's how I found it to be.

Before this tragedy, I never really knew the anguish of grief, and yet, I was surrounded by it. Almost daily it shattered, to some degree, the lives of acquaintances,

friends, and even loved ones. I was sympathetic. I tried
to be understanding. But I never really knew the agony
of their suffering. I searched for words to console them.
I spoke of God's love and quoted Scriptures but, somehow,
I felt that my words were in vain.

Now, I think I know why.

If your body is severely injured, the pain is excruciating,
and remains so until miraculous powers heal the wound.
If not anesthetized, the pain must be endured. I found
that grief can hurt equally, if not more, than physical pain.
It reduced me to a state of shock, and I had to bear the
agony of it, alone. There was no anesthetic. I could not
block it out or ignore it, and I found little relief from
words, answers, or even *prayers.*

Many times, well-meaning words from friends hurt me
more than they helped. Comments such as, "You must
have faith in God," and similar remarks, irritated me. I
saw no relevancy in them. My faith in God had not
dimmed, nor did I have any doubts as to his wisdom or
supremacy. But such faith did not lessen my loss. I winced
when some said, "God had a reason for calling Jody; you
must accept it, Jody won't have to suffer the tragedies of
life that so many of us have faced. We must not question
why God tests us so, he'll not give us more than we can
bear. Think of the joys Jody's having in heaven." And,
the one that bothered me most was, "I understand."

I wanted to scream out, "*Do you?* Tell me you're a father;
that you had a son whom you loved more than yourself;
and that the driver of the car which crushed the last breath
of life from his beautiful young body was arrested for
driving while *drunk!* Tell me all this, and *then* I might
believe you when you say you understand."

Several of my friends who have gone through similar

tragedies told me they experienced this same reaction. In times of grief, it seems that each of us is really no different inside than any other tormented soul. No one else can know how another suffers. Each person's loss *is* the greatest—to *him.* I needed to recognize this and accept it as a part of grief. Or so I told myself, but even that didn't seem to help much.

I hated my reactions to such remarks when they were meant only to comfort me. How could I be so hypersensitive and critical? It seems strange that of all the hundreds of words said to me, few really helped. I shall never forget, however, those who simply sat or walked quietly beside me; who put their arms around me and held me, or cried with me, or told me they loved me. They taught me a lesson in sharing grief.

I shall, also, never forget those who were patient with me when I was difficult to be around; when I acted like I was the only person in the whole world who had lost a loved one; when all I could ever talk about was my son and how no one could understand my loss.

But so many *did* understand. They called or visited us almost daily; included us in their plans and prayers. Took us to their ranches for weekends of hunting and just being together. They invited us into their homes; kept us active in so many wonderful ways. How genuinely understanding and patient they were, and what a terribly lonely place our world would have been without them.

There is something very special about Christian friends, a brotherhood in Christ and a sharing of his love. There's something else—a bond in prayer. I cannot explain it or describe it. I only know that as others prayed for us, we sensed it; we felt it. Through the Holy Spirit, this helped sustain us in those lonely days.

I thought back to that moment when Jesus hung on the cross; when it seemed that even God had deserted him; when in the intense pain of crucifixion, he was all human, like you and me. And in his suffering, he cried out to God, "My God, my God, why have you forsaken me?" It was only for a moment, but in that moment, perhaps he, too, felt all alone.

Through the Holy Spirit, Christ has been but a whisper away from me and, even though I must bear my own pain, *I am not alone.* He, above all, understands the deepest levels of my suffering. In my moment of greatest need, Christ did not *relieve* the pain; he *shared my grief* and comforted me with his infinite love.

Have you ever truly known the love of Christ? It can change your life as it did mine, and James and John, and Andrew and Peter. But don't take my word for it. Pick up a New Testament and read about his love from those far more reliable than I. Read it with your heart, and believe it! For it is true.

I had found my way out of hell; the only way there ever was or ever will be—through God's love. Throughout those horrible hours, it was this love that sustained me; that offered me hope, and comfort, and salvation from despair.

6.
ENCOUNTER WITH SATAN

I spent the second night following Jody's death floating somewhere in the galaxy of space, as detached from the world and reality as an unknown star. I had found a haven in God's love, and was afraid to return to the brutality of life. My body was here but not my mind. I must have communicated with others, but I don't recall it; I must have slept, but I can't separate consciousness from sleep. The only thing I remember is the dawn on Sunday morning.

How depressing it must be to awaken mornings dreading the new day. I have always wanted something exciting to look forward to each morning, and I hate to allow monotony to steal a single day from me. Somehow, someway, as long as God gives me life and health, I'll try to find happiness in it; or so I had always thought.

The only trouble was, I overlooked a force stronger than my own—Satan!

I never admitted it before, but I was not able to accept the Bible's assertion that Satan was a real being—a living spirit. Well, I believe it now. To me, he is no longer a fictitious symbol of evil dreamed up by the writers of the Scriptures; nor is he my base, evil self. He is as real a spirit, to me, as God.

He came into my life that Sunday morning, and he came

as slyly as a fox stealing into the henhouse. He nudged me awake, and softly uttered a single word—*Jody*.

Clang! And I was back in hell.

For the first time, tears came into my eyes, and I could cry. Betsy was asleep beside me and I didn't want to awaken her; being asleep was better than being awake. I rolled over and began to silently pray:

"Oh, Lord, help me. I don't think I can face this day, or the next. I miss Jody so much. . . ."

The reply was deceptively gentle, but somehow, I knew it was not God. *"There, there, go on and cry. I don't see how you can stand such a loss; it's not fair. You've been a good guy all your life, tried to do the right things: obey the laws, believe in God, go to church, be a good neighbor, not drink or run around with other women. Why did this have to happen to you? There are so many bums in the world, why not them? You have a right to pity yourself. It's a lousy, rotten deal."*

I thought, "My mind must be playing tricks on me. I've got to get out of here before I really go nuts."

I quietly slipped out of bed and began dressing. When I arrived in the front part of the house, friends and relatives were already preparing for the day.

It was Sunday, and I had a strong desire to be in my accustomed place, teaching an eleventh grade boys Bible class, but I knew I could not go. I was too shattered mentally, emotionally, and physically; and I began to dread the sympathetic faces of friends and acquaintances. Also, I wondered if they dreaded seeing me. I imagined them uncomfortable in my presence and avoiding me because they didn't know what to say. The aura of suffering and death seemed to surround me like a plague. Maybe, I had such feelings because I remembered having similiar ones when I was with friends in mourning. Perhaps I just imagined it all.

I began to think of Ivy and the Hagens and their lonely vigil. I asked Betsy if she could go with me to visit them, but she didn't think we should both leave the house, so I drove off alone.

At the hospital, Mr. and Mrs. Hagens confirmed reports I had been getting: the doctors held no hope for Ivy. Soon there would be two gone, and the world would not be nearly as bright a place.

On the way home, it all welled up inside me, and I started screaming out my rage in filthy profanity. It was my way of blowing off steam, directed at no one. No, that's not altogether true; at that moment, I hated everything.

In my raving frenzy, I heard the voice again, egging me on, amplifying my phrases, filling in words I couldn't find; on and on, until my screaming gradually ebbed into choking sobs.

I stopped the car, put my head down on the steering wheel, and wanted to die.

Once again, there was that strange, tempting voice: *"You poor thing. Let me help you. Go on and cry, then let's go out and raise hell. Better yet, start up the car and let's go for a ride—a fast ride. Put the top down, and let the wind blow in your face. Feel the thrill of speed, the excitement, the danger. Be alive! Live! Come on, I'll help you forget your troubles."*

It was as clear as if the words had been spoken aloud, and the temptation was exciting beyond description. I hated myself for being so square. I wanted to kick convention in the face, and spit on the whole stinking world.

I put the top down, started the engine, and jammed

my foot on the accelerator. The tires screamed as the car roared forward, and I heard a wild insane laughter that seemed to come from my tortured soul. But I wasn't laughing. I was crying! And, through the tears that blinded my eyes, I saw Jody's face; and I was ashamed.

In the early drafts of this manuscript, I left out most of the details of this episode because it seemed overly dramatic. What a horrible experience it was, and traumatic beyond words. It was the first time I was aware of Satan's intervention in my life, and it came very close to leading me straight into hell!

I wondered why I had never before had such a personal encounter with Satan. Where had he been, and why this sudden appearance? And then it dawned on me.

Up to now, my life had been without real tragedy; a nice smooth excursion on a beautiful highway with only minor detours. I realized my relationship with God had been that way: a well-ordered, Sunday church services, "Now I lay me down to sleep," type of relationship. I had no real need of God. I believed in him, I was thankful to him for my blessings, but I really didn't *know* him. I thought I did, but I didn't—not really.

Following this tragedy, I found myself begging God for comfort and, out of his boundless love, he comforted me.

I recognized now, that, as my dependence on God grew, and my love became stronger, I created the one situation which Satan could not tolerate. So long as I merely *believed* in God, I offered no real threat to Satan. But as I came to really *worship* God at a deeper level than I had ever previously experienced; as I committed more and more of myself to his will; as my total dependence on him grew; and, as he responded with infinite compassion and love, Satan found it necessary to bring all of his guile, cunning, and evil to bear, in a relentless assault on my mind.

Since that time, I seldom have moments with God when Satan is not also present. Sometimes I feel that he is closer to me than God, and perhaps it is because I live in his domain. He forever tempts me to do the things I hate, to think thoughts for which I am ashamed—to ignore my God.

I don't know how anyone can successfully withstand his temptations alone. I cannot. It is only when my mind is attuned to God that I can resist Satan.

When I had gained control of myself, I started the car and drove on, my mind a caldron of emotions, my nerves raw and exposed. I drove aimlessly, not wanting to face people in my present state. I tried to be brave and courageous but could not control my self-pity. Finally, with a great deal of effort, I screwed on the best face I could manage, and went home.

Coming back among people was a real ordeal. I should have gone off somewhere and stayed until I could sort things out in my mind. I wasn't fit company for anyone. Ugliness and bitterness began to creep into my mind.

Several times, during the afternoon of that second day, I sought solitude, and wanted to be in God's presence. I found neither. The night was dark and lonely, and I dreaded the coming day.

My fears were justified. As I think back to that day when we buried our son, my hands tremble, my jaws tighten, and a lump rises in my throat. I recall the events as from a horror story—a play enacted in the subconscious. I cannot bring myself to recount the funeral service in this narrative, nor do I feel it important to the message. There was one incident, however:

Several days after the service, a guidance counselor, from

the high school Jody attended, came to visit Betsy. She told her of the steady stream of students who had come to her office. They were searching for answers as to why God allowed such tragic deaths to happen.

She said, "I've spent most of my time crying with them; but there was one girl who told me something I thought you should know. She had attended Jody's funeral and said, 'I had become so bitter about many adults, with their coldness and indifference. But when I looked around me, I saw many of those same people crying; people whom I thought didn't care about anyone in the whole world. There they were, crying and caring. And I thought how wrong I had been.'"

My Savior was crucified, and on the third day he arose; and because he did, my son, whose body was buried on the third day, shall also live. This sure knowledge, together with the assurance that there will come the time when I'll again know him and love him, is the wellspring of the hope that brings light into my dark hours.

7.
JODY

Jody's death has made me realize what a fragile, fleeting thing life is. Do you remember the story of the boy who, holding a tiny bird in his hand, went to a wise man and asked, "Father, is the bird I hold alive or dead?" The wise man replied, "As you wish it, my son; you hold its destiny in your hand."

It seems to me that life is like that: a flickering flame, held in the cold hand of death.

One squeeze, and the flame is no more. And, in the trailing wisp of smoke, the love, the dreams, the seemingly endless tomorrows, of those who survive, vanish into nothingness; and only a haunting, lonely emptiness remains among the treasured memories of yesterday.

Memories—they are all that remain of my son. They dance in and out of the shadows of my mind, glow for a moment like a firefly in the night, and then disappear; only to be replaced by another and another and another.

Each time I freeze a picture, I get a different view, each one more painful than the last.

I've never been able to look at the thousands of old pictures and movies we have of our children. The sweetness of those bygone days and children, now grown, is far too poignant for me to recall without a deep, longing sadness.

One day, walking down the hall, I passed Jody's room;

and Satan nudged me toward the door. I resisted, knowing that to go in would only bring back the memories; but the temptation was too strong and I entered the room.

Walking toward the desk, I spied his scrapbook lying unopened on the top. I closed my eyes and turned away, but Satan said, *"Open it. Don't you hunger to see him?"*

I hesitated, torn with indecision, and then half reluctantly, half eagerly, began to turn the pages. The years rolled back. . . .

What a beautiful child he was: large, brown eyes, black hair, and skin the natural golden tan of sunshine. He was a sensitive, kind, considerate lad, endowed with an inquisitive, sharp mind, and a keen ear for music. He played the piano and organ by ear and sang beautiful harmony. Because his life was so well organized and disciplined, he found time for a wide range of participation in the arts, music, sports, debate, and just plain fun.

How much he had accomplished for one so young: There was a picture of him in the Little Theatre production, "Stop the World." We were amazed at the sensitive performance he gave as everyman's son.

And, as a Little Leaguer: He didn't especially like baseball, but played it for my sake; played for seven years and made the All-Stars in both Little League and Pony League.

And football: my "All American," playing quarterback. My, how big he looked in that uniform—and so tough! But he wasn't, really; he was too gentle for football, and after playing two years in Junior high school, told me one day, "Dad, I don't want to play football anymore; I don't like to hurt people." I understood and told him to make the decision himself; whatever he decided was fine with me; and it was.

And basketball—now there was a game he loved. At fifteen, he was six feet, two inches tall. I'll never forget the afternoon of the evening he was killed. He had only been practicing with the high school team for one week and his coach asked him to begin work with the varsity— how proud and excited he was.

And all those happy pictures: at camp in the Hill Country of Texas, birthday parties and family outings, and, scattered among the pictures, blue ribbons and awards and mementos of a rich, full, young life.

And now where were all those dreams? Buried in a cold, wind-swept cemetery.

The tears welled in my eyes and I said, "Oh, God, is it really true? Is he really dead? Gone forever?"

I don't know why I asked; of course he was dead! I knew that. Gone forever? Well, I had the answer to that too, if I believed. But I pressed on:

"Why Jody, God? He was so young, still a child in many ways. He missed so much in life. Why?"

I sensed his answer in a return question, "WHAT DID YOU SAY TO YOUR CHILDREN WHEN THEY ASKED QUESTIONS BEYOND THEIR UNDER-STANDING?"

"I just told them they were too young, and someday they would understand. It didn't seem to bother them; they went on happily to something else."

"THEY DID NOT DEMAND AN ANSWER?"

"No Lord, I guess they trusted me. Lord, when I ask why, over and over again, does that mean I don't trust you?"

But then the voice I'd heard in the car interrupted: *"Hey man. You have a right to ask why he took your son."*

"Why did you call Jody, God?"

No answer. . . .

"Did you call Jody, God?"

Still no answer, only more of Satan's prodding:

"He must have, he's God. He controls the universe and everything that goes on in it."

Then I remembered God's sentence upon Adam and Eve and all their descendants; instead of obedience to his will, they wanted to be like Gods, to know good from evil. From that day, death and sorrow has been man's lot.

"Are you trying to tell me, Lord, that Jody's death was just a part of life?—it seems a shame. It doesn't seem fair to him. He had so many talents; I thought you had special plans for him."

I could almost hear him say, "I DID."

"You say that as though you're sad too, as though you share my grief," I said.

Once again I heard Satan's sarcasm: *"Yeah, sure, we're all sad; and in the meantime, what about Jody? He's dead, lost his life, and for what?"*

"I don't have to worry about Jody. He's with God," I said. "I grieve because he died so young and missed many of the wonderful experiences of life. He never knew the thrill of kissing a girl, or being in love, or marriage, or driving a car on his own, or building a home, or fatherhood, or business, or the thousands of joys and challenges and victories and defeats of adulthood. He worked and studied so hard in preparation, and now it all seems wasted—all for nothing.

"But maybe not! I don't know, I'll just have to trust God. I can't trust you. You bring me no comfort, no peace, nothing. Go away!"

"I understand," Satan said. *"You miss your son. I know*

how you feel. Remember the great times you had with him? How proud you must have been of him. If you could only have him back—your son."

"Oh, God!" I cried, "I want my boy back!"

I seemed to hear him say, "FOR HOW LONG?"

And I remembered when Jody was born. As with all my children, I felt like God was saying, "HERE IS MY SON, WHOSE BODY WAS BORN OF YOUR FLESH; GIVE HIM A NAME, LOVE HIM, AND CARE FOR HIS NEEDS UNTIL IT IS TIME FOR HIM TO DEPART FROM YOU UNTO HIS OWN LIFE. BUT DO NOT FORGET THAT HE IS *MY* SON."

"I forgot," I said. "I'm acting like I expected to have him forever; he was your son, Father."

Instantly, Satan interrupted again. *"Phooey! He wasn't God's son, he was **your** son. You gave him life, not God. Remember how much like you he was? You were his father, but you didn't protect him. You should not have let him ride his bicycle at night. You should have kept a closer eye on him. But no, you turned him over to God."*

"I couldn't follow him everywhere," I said. "You can't keep an active fifteen-year-old boy in a glass bottle. Overprotection would have stifled him and destroyed our relationship. Besides, he wanted to 'try his wings.' He needed to fly."

"Quit kidding yourself and face the facts," Satan said. *"Jody was very young, and you knew the dangers of riding a bicycle at night on busy streets. You blew it! You let him down. You're the cause of his death—you and your negligence."*

"Don't say that," I cried, "it's not so! I discussed safety with him several times. Once I suggested to him that he ride his bicycle facing the traffic and he said, 'I can't do that, Dad, it's against the law.' What could I say to that?

"No, that's not why he was killed. He was killed because he was unlucky enough to be on the same road as a drunk driver at the wrong time. Nothing can save you from drunk drivers—nothing or no one!"

"Not even God?" Satan asked.

"That's right, not even God!" I said. "At least, he didn't save Jody. Oh, God, why did you let Jody be killed?"

"I don't hear any answer—do you?" Satan asked.

"No. . . ."

"Why are you so easy on God? If it were me, you'd raise all kinds of hell!"

"Leave me alone," I said.

"Gon'na cop out again, eh?" Satan sneered.

"No, I'm not gon'na cop out, but I won't blame God either, and that's what you want me to say."

"You could have prayed for God to protect him," Satan slyly suggested.

"I did," I murmured.

"Perhaps he was too busy." Satan replied. *"He has so many followers, you know. Sometimes he just can't get around to all the prayers. Prayer is O.K., especially if you follow it with some good old-fashioned actions on your own part. It makes you wonder, sometimes, whether you really need God at all, doesn't it?"*

"No, I need God," I said.

"Why?" he asked. *"The book of Genesis says that Adam and Eve were told that if they ate the forbidden fruit, they would be like gods. They ate it, and all mankind has been god-like since. You're your own god. Command your own destiny. Look to yourself for your own salvation."*

"You and I both know who told Eve that," I said, "and you've been trying to sell that line ever since. Go crawl off in your hole and leave me alone. Why is it that you're always around bugging me when I'm hurt and confused and most vulnerable?"

"I care for you, that's why," Satan added, with what I was sure must have been a grin.

"Yeah, you care for me all right," I told him; "you'll care for me straight into hell!"

For days, those thoughts haunted me. Had I been negligent as a parent? Had I failed to protect my son? Was I partially to blame for his death? These, and similar self-incrimination doubts must have plagued parents for ages.

I am convinced that questions and doubts such as these serve absolutely no purpose. In fact they may have a selfish motivation. I am no psychologist, but I sense in such self-accusation, a morbid desire to ease my pain by whipping myself. I don't understand it, but it's unhealthy for me. And even if I were somehow to blame, what earthly difference would it make? Can I change the past? Can I bring back my son? Can I relive that fateful September evening when, after I had soldered the broken wire on his bicycle lights, I watched him ride off into eternity?

Oh, God! How I have wished I *could* have back that one moment in time. . . .

In desperation, I have screamed aloud to God. But God knows, even as wise parents also know, that you cannot talk or reason with a hysterical child. You must first take him into your arms and love him.

Out of my loneliness, I have sought my Savior's love. I have tortured myself with incriminating guilt, envied those whose sons still lived, inwardly criticized friends who offended me with words meant only to comfort, wanted my son back, regretted the times I ignored him, pitied myself for having to miss those exciting parts of his life, sobbed in agony for him because he did not want to die, and, wished, wished, wished, for things that can never be.

8.
YESTERDAY

Yesterday—those good 'ole days—oh, how I loved them. Like a broken record, they play, over and over in the caverns of my mind.

My childhood days of wonder and discovery: of raindrops glistening on pine needles, and the flat clang of the streetcar bell on cobblestone streets; the rousing call of roosters signaling the sun; the lonesome whistle of long freight trains heading for the open prairie; sweet milk with swirls of golden cream; buttermilk biscuits; the sound of voices; the warmth of laughter; and the sweetness of belonging and being loved. I loved my mother and father dearly, and somehow sensed that I was the "apple of their eye."

By the time I was five, I could count by twos. Mother was impressed and absolutely convinced that I was a child prodigy, so she promptly enrolled me in school. I loved it in September, endured it in January, and despised it in May. The last day of school each year was so exhilarating that, on my way home, I hardly brushed the ground as I flew along on wings of joy.

Summers were an escape from the adult world of discipline and a return to the magic world of childhood—a world of homemade ice cream, circuses, and cotton candy. It was too good to be real.

The only trouble with starting school so young was my age. When the other guys wanted to play baseball, I was clumsy at catching a ball. When they became bold enough to derail the trolley on streetcars, I was chicken. When they started eying girls, I could not understand why. If I sought out friends in lower grades, my own classmates made fun of me. I became a sort of in-betweener and missed out on a lot of social fun. But it forced me to study, and I entered Rice University when I was barely sixteen.

I don't think my grades were good enough for Rice but my dad talked the registrar into giving me a chance; I always knew dad was the world's greatest salesman.

I began to see the light when I was fifteen and tried, in my stumbling way, to make friends with certain girls. But no self-respecting high school senior girl would even say hello to a fifteen-year-old, so I promptly gave it up again.

Later, when I became a college freshman, I had added prestige, but not with college girls. I went back to the high school seniors, but my lack of maturity overshadowed my stature.

As a college sophomore, I regularly made the high school dances and it was there that I met Betsy. Now it worked in reverse; because of my *lofty* position, I frightened her, and she was afraid to go out with me. What a mess!

A year later, at a Rice dance, I saw her again. When I cut in, she said, "Hello, *George.*" I'd really made an impression; my name is *Frank.*

I have never cared to relive my life but, oh how I enjoyed those college days; they rest sweet in my memory.

Betsy was the queen of the campus to me. I shall never forget what a vision of loveliness she was, among the pink azaleas and white dogwood trees of the Rice May Fete

Court.

During this period, I was beating my brains out studying, while she was involved in all sorts of activities. She even managed to be elected vice-president of her senior class.

I received a bachelor of arts degree at the end of my senior year, and returned the following year for a bachelor of science degree in architecture.

After five years of college, I was twenty years old, had two earned degrees, and the best looking, best built, sweetest fiancée in the entire world.

So what did I do? Why I joined the Army Air Corps the next day, naturally!

Upon Betsy's graduation a year later, I married my girl; and then spent three more years helping to stop the Germans and Japanese from trying to conquer the world, my beloved land included. I hated the regimentation of army life, and received my discharge with the same wild enthusiasm of those childhood summer vacations.

After the war, Betsy and I wanted children badly, but it was not the Lord's will. She had several miscarriages, and we were becoming quite concerned about it. We moved from Houston to Corpus Christi in 1947, and I entered the construction business with my dad.

In the early part of 1949, we drove to Monterrey, Mexico, for a weekend with another couple. While there, we visited Horsetail Falls and rode small Mexican burros to the top of the falls. It was a laughing, bumpy ride.

A few days after we returned home, Betsy discovered that she was well along in pregnancy.

Our first child, Patti, was born October 1, 1949.

Since that event, I have never failed to associate riding burros with having babies; surely there can't be any connection, and I don't recommend it, but well—when you've tried everything else . . .?

After 1949, having additional children was a bi-annual event for us. Nancy was born in 1951, and Terry in 1953. Because we thought three children was enough, we avoided the burros in 1955; I'm sorry now that we did.

Jody, our last, was born in 1957. By then, we had become dedicated parents, and our life was largely built around the children.

I was busy making money and providing all the luxuries I thought our family needed: a swimming pool in the back yard, a Cadillac in the garage, and a live-in maid.

The term *maid* needs explaining. Several weeks before Jody was born, we were looking for someone, and a young woman came to see us about the job. Her name was Sara Flores from the small, neighboring city of Robstown. She went to work for us shortly thereafter, and has remained ever since, but not as a maid. She's been more like a second mother to our children, a friend to Betsy and me, and a full-fledged member of our family. We all love her, and are grateful for having known her these seventeen years.

Betsy continued the participation in community affairs she had begun in school and college. She became president of the City Federation of Women's Clubs, a member of the Junior League, active in various phases of our church, and involved in countless school and social functions; they were busy, happy days for her.

Not to be outdone, I too, became involved. I was ordained a deacon in a Baptist church, elected president of the Rotary Club, became director of a financial institution, trustee of a college, director of various community, business, and professional organizations, and a "so called" pillar of the community.

In 1961, my brother Bob and I merged our businesses

into the Peerman Corporation: a firm engaged in architecture, construction, land planning, subdividing, and general real estate development. Because of our mutual love and respect for each other, it has been a very rare and precious partnership. It is rewarding to drive throughout our city and state and see subdivisions, buildings, country clubs, townhouses, apartments, homes, and developments of all kinds that have, directly or indirectly, been a product of our creativity and efforts.

In terms of worldly goods, prestige, and social standing, we had more than our share. There were very few luxuries that I denied myself or my family, and we loved it!

Our two daughters were selected as dutchesses in the Las Donas de La Corte, Buccaneer Ball, held annually in Corpus Christi. In addition, they were each presented to society, as debutantes, by The Order of De Pineda. What a proud papa I was, and how much I loved each one: Patti, with her dark hair and blue eyes and our precious "red head," Nancy.

Terry, our first son, was an outstanding athlete in baseball and tennis, and was awarded a tennis scholarship to Baylor University. No man ever had four finer children, nor loved them more.

So the days passed. We lived our lives fully, conscious of our blessing, oblivious to the risks that surrounded us, and secure in the belief that God would watch over us.

In the last few years, preceeding Jody's death, we recognized that our life-style was changing.

First Patti was married; then Nancy. And Terry had gone away to college. We were reluctantly adapting from a home and life built around children, to an *empty nest.* This too is a part of life and we accepted it, but we dearly loved the precious years when they were all at home. Their problems, their joys, their activities, their friends, were all a part of our lives, and we lived vicariously through each one.

I don't mean to imply that we resented their growing away. We wanted each of them to know the joys of life that we had known. We thrilled as they found their wings and flew eagerly into the world. But we were human enough to feel a little sorry for ourselves. We consoled such self-pity with the knowledge that we still had Jody, with his wonderful high school and college years ahead. Such consolation was short-lived.

Upon his death, Betsy and I faced the double trauma of his personal loss, plus the sudden realization that the big house, once full of happy, laughing children, was suddenly quiet and terribly empty. We could not walk among the rooms or through the grounds without hearing thousands of echos from the past. There was no avoiding it, no escape.

It somehow seems strange to me that, even though Jody's death was almost constantly in our thoughts, we could not talk with each other about it; it hurt too much, I guess, and words couldn't relieve the pain. So each of us bore our grief alone, and in our own way, and we waited upon time.

During this waiting period, we sensed God's working in our lives. I found myself becoming more aware of how precious Patti, Nancy, and Terry really were.

Each one is a special person, and has carved her or his own niche in my heart. One can not fill the niche of another, nor ever replace the loss. So it was with Jody; it would have been the same with Patti, or Nancy, or Terry. I have loved all four equally; I would grieve equally over the loss of any one.

It has also been true, that, I have thrilled in each one's achievements, joys, and triumphs; have shared the disappointments and pains.

Patti, our firstborn, was a child to warm the heart of any parent; happy, laughing, and carefree in her own charming way, she brings pure pleasure into our lives and occupies a place in my heart that is hers alone.

Nancy fulfilled our desire for another daughter, but in a delightful and surprising way. Born with red hair, she has the temperament to match. With her, life is exciting and full of spice, never dull. She may occasionally "get my goat," but her capacity for love and devotion is like pure gold, and I adore her.

Any man whom God has blessed with a son understands how I feel about Terry. For days after his birth, I was as excited and proud as a man could be. My first son! Twenty-one years have gone by, now, and he has added a deep love to that joy and pride. In many ways, I relive parts of my own life through him, and find it wonderful.

Betsy and I noticed that, where before, we had been the "rock" upon which our children could lean in times of trouble, they now saw us broken and confused and human in our weakness. I was thankful for the times we had discouraged their childish worship of us, suggesting that they put their trust in God, for he alone would never fail them.

Sensing the depth of our grief after Jody's death, they found themselves able to minister to our needs, and were magnificent in their response. For days, Patti and Nancy did not leave us alone. They readjusted their lives around us. Terry called from college almost every evening. Their love was so genuine and gentle and their attentions so sweet that they slowly brought back the smiles to our faces and songs of thanksgiving from our hearts.

I began to think back to that day in Houston when it all began—the day Betsy and I were married.

The temperature was around seventy degrees, and as I waited in the pastor's study, I felt like I was freezing to death: shaking all over, teeth chattering, and hardly able to speak. I was just plain *scared!* Our sympathetic pastor lit the heater, and suggested that I warm myself before entering the sanctuary for the ceremony. He and my father got a real kick out of watching me shiver. Preachers and fathers have probably laughed at scared, young bridegrooms throughout the ages.

I have often wondered what I was afraid of; I wanted to marry Betsy more than anything else in the world. It might have been the subconscious fear of responsibilities, of being a husband and father—the head of a new family. It could have been something else; the fear of loving someone so much that I could become vulnerable. In my case, I suspect it was the latter.

I shall never forget the panic that came over me when Patti, our older daughter, was eighteen months old. I sat in the doctor's waiting room holding her, deeply concerned because of her high fever. Suddenly she went into convulsions, and for a few agonizing seconds, I watched as the spasms wracked her tiny body. I thought I was going to die, and surely would have, had not the nurse quickly taken her from my arms.

As they began to treat her, I frantically paced the room, mumbling, "Why did I ever get married? Oh, why did I ever get married?" Now I was twice as vunerable; and with the arrival of each child, my vunerability increased.

But I discovered that life is like that—the "Name of the Game," so to speak. It seems to me that each time we open our hearts to someone in love, we give away a part of ourselves; and in the giving we discover the *fullness* of life. How terribly lonely life would be if we lived it being afraid to love, for fear of being hurt; and how much we would miss of the sweetness.

Even though we had Jody for only fifteen years, I would not have traded a single day with him for ten lifetimes without him.

God promised me life *more abundantly,* and he has fulfilled that promise. He did not, however, promise me exemption from pain, suffering, and grief, which is a part of life. My trials and tribulations had been so few that I had become lulled into a false feeling of immunity.

Occasionally, in moments when the sweetness of success or pride in my beloved children seemed almost too good to be true, I would wonder how anyone could deserve such intense happiness; and then, a nagging fear would come over me. . . .

I remembered sitting in the audience during Jody's junior high school graduation ceremonies. He was awarded his third annual certificate for outstanding scholastic achievement, having made all A's for three years. Following the awards, he performed a lead role in the school's musical production. He stood so tall and handsome, and my heart swelled with pride.

After the performance, I went to him and said, "Buddy, I can't tell you how proud I am of you. You've accomplished so much more than your dad was ever able to do. You really are 'something else.' " It embarrassed him, and he smiled that shy but pleased smile of his.

I congratulated him, also, on the fine compliment his principal had paid him, when he handed him his award. And in his unassuming way, he said, "But Dad, I wish he hadn't singled me out. There were several others on the platform who did as well or better than I did."

As I left the school that day, I'll never forget thinking, "He's too good to be true," and perhaps he was.

"Yesterday—those good 'ole days . . ."

Wait a minute! Listen to those words again . . .

"Yesterday—those good 'ole days . . ."

Do you hear it—the lie? No wonder Satan keeps whispering it over and over. The sly 'ole fox! He's done it again; been doing it for years and I never suspected.

Don't you see? It's the *good 'ole days* bit. The past is better than the present; yesterday was better than today. I have troubles today, but yesterday life was a bowl of cherries, the world was my oyster, my cup overflowed. Phooey! I knew all kinds of yesterdays: wonderful, good, fair, bad, and horrible! But for me to say that they were all better than today is not necessarily so.

Was my life better as a child than as a teenager? I didn't think so then; I wanted to grow up so badly I often lied about my age. And yet, I loved my childhood.

Was my life better as a teenager than as an adult? Those teenage years, with all their trauma, emotion, and decisions are certainly not ones I would like to relive. No, they were not better and, yet, I had a ball!

Was my life better before I married Betsy? Well, let me put it this way. Knowing what I've known since marrying her, I wish I had done it two years earlier.

Was my life better before each child was born; before Patti, Nancy, Terry, Jody? No it was not. I wish, now, we'd had two or three more children; I loved parenthood, and never wanted it to end.

So the past was not better than the present and I should not let it bother me.

But Satan was not to be so easily denied, *"Wait a minute,"* he said, *"you didn't finish your analysis. Is your life better now than it was before Jody was killed?"*

I could not answer.

"Well, is it? Come on tell us the truth."

"No," I said, reluctantly.

"Well, well," he said, *"you just blew your whole argument. Yesterday was better than today."*

"You miss the point," I said. Jody was only a part of my life, a wonderful, irreplaceable part. His death was a horrible nightmare, and through it, I shared with all men one of life's deepest human experiences—grief. I will never forget it, nor ever fully recover from it. Neither will my life ever again be the same. But life is like that, constantly moving on, from one phase to another—the relentless march of time. I wouldn't want it any other way.

"I wish I had him back. No, I'd give almost *anything* to have him back! But it can't be. And I must not waste today wishing for impossible things.

"Jody would not want that. If he were back for a moment, I know what he would say. Something like, 'Come on, Dad, hook 'em up; life's too short; believe me, I know. Get back in the game and give it all you've got. We never were quitters, you and I, so don't let one set-back get you down. Show 'em what you're made of; hit one for me.' "

And, maybe, in my stumbling way, that's what I'm trying to do—hit one for Jody.

9.
BETSY

In Ephesians, Paul says, that, through marriage, a man and woman shall become one flesh. Even he could not understand it and simply stated it as a divine fact—the two shall be one.

I don't understand it either, but I believe it. Betsy is so much a part of me that when I'm separated from her, I sense an incompleteness, a loneliness that no person or place can fill. I think of her as a part of myself: As I love myself, I also love her; as I am sometimes angry with myself, I am occasionally angry with her; as I do not completely understand myself, neither do I completely understand her. It's amazing that two lives can be so inter-mingled—amazing and wonderful!

It has been that way with us for thirty years, with a single exception.

For a period of time after Jody was killed, Betsy and I spun *separately* through the maelstrom of grief like tumbling leaves before the storm. For the first time neither of us could help the other. Friends suggested it was because we shared the same loss. But it seems to me it was more than that. Granted we shared the same loss, but why couldn't we share it together? Why did we go off in our own little corners and grieve alone?

We could not seem to synchronize our moods. Many

times, when she was up, I'd be down, and vice versa. Once
while driving home, I saw a boy on a bicycle, ahead of
me.

Satan said, *"Look! There's Jody!"*

My heart raced; he did look exactly like Jody. My crazy
mind knew better, but all kinds of emotions swirled around
in my head. I had passed the boy but Satan kept on:

"Stop! Let him pass. Are you sure it isn't Jody?"

I couldn't keep from stopping. The boy rode pass and
I felt like an idiot. It made me furious and I drove on,
so blindingly mad I could have crushed my teeth into bits.

You can imagine my mood when I arrived home and
there was Betsy, happily standing at the door, waiting to
welcome me and share her love. . . .

And there were other times when I was writing or work-
ing on my model railroad. Suddenly I would wonder where
Betsy was. Once I found her in our bedroom, curled up
on a corner of the bed, her eyes bloodshot from weeping.
I sat beside her, not saying anything, trying to let her know
I understood and cared.

She turned to me and asked, "Why? Why? Why?"

Her lifelong faith was built around a God who protected
his own. She was so sure of that because of the many
times he had answered her prayers. But now, her mind
searched blindly for answers.

"Why did God allow this to happen?" she cried. "Why
to *Jody*? He endowed him with so many talents, and then,
to let him die at fifteen! Why? It's impossible!" She could
find absolutely no logic in it.

And what about her prayer? "Were they in vain?" she
asked. "Futile, wasted effort?

"What does a mother do? Pray that God's will be done,
and then, assume that he caused or allowed Jody's death

for a reason of his own which I can't understand? If such is the case," she concluded, "then it was useless for me to pray for Jody's protection, or for any other of my loved ones.' In fact, why pray at all?" she said.

Prayer had been such a vital part of her fundamental faith—her security. Was her understanding of it all wrong? She had always believed that God controls everything that happens in this world of ours; or he could if he so desired.

"If that is so," she said, "then why did he cause or allow this? What earthly reason could he have had, or heavenly either, for that matter? If he doesn't control everything," she said, "then the whole, horrible thing was just a senseless accident, and Jody died for nothing! Oh, God!" she cried.

And where did she go from here? With this part of her security stripped away was the remainder of her life to be a constant endless fear? If that were the case, then, no thank you! She didn't care to live like that; getting sick to her stomach every time she heard the screaming wail of a siren; dreading to answer the telephone when it rang late at night; watching her loved ones leave, each time, with a knot of fear in her throat.

"Oh, God! God!" she cried. "Help me!"

At first, such questions on Betsy's part came as a surprise to me. It may have been because I had never heard her so openly question God. Her faith had always been the stronger, the more unshakable. I was the rebel, the independent thinker, the one who questioned the church, the Scriptures, anything that didn't seem logical in my own egotistical assurance of right and wrong.

Later, as Betsy seemed to withdraw more and more in her loneliness it concerned me, frightened me, and threatened my security. She had been such a stabilizing influence in my life and I needed that stability. She couldn't crack-up! Not Betsy! Not now! I had to do something. . . .

In typical fashion, I put the 'ole brain to work, and in short order, had it all figured out. (How easy it is to solve other people's problems.)

First, Betsy felt like God had let her down. Secondly, her concepts of prayer had been shaken. The solution was quite clear. She needed to trust God.

Several nights later, I tenderly brought up the subject, told her of my concern, and offered my brilliant conclusion. I suppose I expected my words of wisdom to change her despair to hope, her sadness to joy, and wash away all her questions and doubts. *It didn't quite work out that way.*

She listened patiently, looked at me with tears rimming her eyes, and said, "I know that, but it still doesn't answer my questions, and life is just not as much fun anymore."

It broke my heart. I wanted so much to help her, to make everything all right. How helpless I felt. . . .

So I turned to God. I prayed for guidance and wisdom. I prayed for him to redirect my thinking, to give me the words and show me the way to help this one whom I loved so dearly. In my conceit I thought God needed *me* to be his instrument. How stupid! He was Betsy's Lord, too, and he loved her more than I. He knew her needs more than I ever could, and would supply those needs in his own time.

I was right in a way. Not only did *Betsy* need to trust him, but so did I.

Realizing this, I began to pray for the Holy Spirit to fill the aching loneliness within us, to comfort us, to love us so much that we could come to know nothing else was really important; and then we would realize that *his* love was sufficient, even in this terrible ordeal.

And so, we turned to God together. What else could

we do? I didn't have any answers to her questions, nor did she have any to mine. I decided I might as well stop kidding myself. As long as I live on this earth, the only things I'll *ever* know about the divine mysteries of God are those truths he reveals to me through revelation and the Holy Scriptures. The Scriptures say that he created me, loves me, sent his Son to die for me, and is sufficient for *all* my needs. I either believe that and trust him, or I don't.

And, incidentally, that's enough for me. I seem to spend entirely too much time asking questions. Trying to understand the infinite, with my simple, finite mind, seeking answers to mysteries which I can't handle, yet. Someday I may understand; but not now. I don't have the mental capacity; I'm still a child to God.

I have concluded that there is really only one relevant question, for me: *Do I believe and trust God?* When I can say in truth and honesty and faith, "I do!" then all other questions about life and death are unnecessary and tend to belie my trust.

But for me, real trust demands a deep faith and a willingness to surrender my will to the divine will of God. Let me illustrate what that can mean.

I stood in the hospital one day, beside a brokenhearted mother. Her son had been critically injured in an auto accident. Her eyes revealed the intense strain of her ordeal, and yet, there was a look of peace about her.

She told me of her initial fears and hopes and prayers when she had first heard the tragic news of her son's accident. Then she said, "On the way to the hospital, I suddenly realized I was praying, 'My will be done.' But I thought, what if I pray, 'Thy will be done' and his will is that my son die! Oh, God, that would be like praying for my son's death. Have you ever had to make such a decision?" she asked.

I shook my head, and she continued, "I can't tell you how many times I have so easily prayed, 'Not my will, but Thy will, O Lord.' I don't think I ever understood what I was really saying. But this time it was the hardest decision I had to make in my entire life; but I made it! And, with my heart in my throat, I prayed, 'Lord I trust you! *Thy* will be done, in this day, as in every other day of my life.'"

"When I had done this," she said, "a great feeling of peace descended upon me, and I was ready for whatever happened. God is so much wiser than I, and I have to trust him."

It was God's will that her son live. I knew God had allowed me the rare privilege that day of witnessing an example of real faith. She would have been all right had her son not lived. I knew it then, and am even more sure of it now.

It was God's will that our son not live; and in his tragic death, we discovered what it is like to accept those things over which we have no control and to trust in God's mercy to see us through. It has been harder to accept than I ever imagined possible.

Gradually, as Betsy and I have been able to place more and more trust in our Lord, we have rediscovered that oneness of spirit, mind, and body that we knew before.

While working at the office the other day, I suddenly had a hunger to hear her voice and called home. She answered the phone with that familiar, "Hello," that sounds so sweet to my ears. I said, "Everything's all right now. . . ." And she laughed with complete understanding and love.

10.
RETRIBUTION

This is a difficult chapter for me to write. I must go back to the evening of the tragedy.

On our way to the hospital, my mind was tormented with all kinds of cruel thoughts: How did it happen? Who was to blame? Were the kids careless? Was Jody killed instantly? Did he lie on the roadside all alone, his body broken, his lifeblood draining away? Was he in pain, afraid, and trying to call out to his mother and dad? What thoughts flashed across his mind at the moment before impact? Did he see the car? Did he know he was going to be hit? Did he cry out? Scream? Freeze? Try to leap clear? Or did he even know what hit him?

To this day, I don't know any of the details as to how he died, and it's better that I don't. I prefer to think that he had no warning and was killed instantly, without pain or suffering.

When we arrived at the emergency entrance to the hospital, the first person I met was the police officer who investigated the accident. I only recall the portion of his conversation in which he said, "Mr. Peerman, the skid marks indicated the kids were riding close to the curb, and were struck from the rear. We arrested the driver of the car for driving while intoxicated."

I asked who the driver was, and the officer gave me

his name. I don't know why I asked; perhaps it was the fear that it might be someone I knew. My grief was too intense to be thinking logically.

But I did not forget the man's name; it haunted me throughout the following days. I had all kinds of questions: What did he look like? What kind of person was he? Why did he hit them? Could he have avoided it? How drunk was he? Was he speeding? On and on, the questions plagued me. . . .

Little by little, I heard scattered reports: According to the law, he was too drunk to drive. The skid marks placed his speed at the time of the crash at approximately fifty-nine miles an hour. The accident occurred in a thirty mile an hour speed zone. The district attorney's office was preparing a charge against him of murder without malice.

After hearing the evidence, the grand jury returned such an indictment. My suspicions and fears were justified. Now, the law was saying he had murdered my son!

Satan had been saying it for days; murmuring accusations, prodding me, trying to build hatred and revenge.

With the law having confirmed it I began thinking, "He killed them! He dulled his senses with booze, got in his car, and ran down two innocent kids. He should pay!" What did it matter that he had done so *without malice.* Were Jody and Ivy any less *dead?*

But what could I do? Search him out and shoot him? How ridiculous! This isn't the "Old West," and besides, I could not shoot anyone. I reminded myself of a braying jackass who had just been shot-gunned.

Who was I trying to kid? If that man owed a debt to society, it was up to the law to collect it. And vengeance belongs to God—not me! I don't know anything about vengeance. What vengeance would have satisfied me? I was trying to play God, and was miserably equipped for the role. I felt like a fool, and prayed to God to forgive me.

But Satan would have none of it, *"Get off your knees!"* he said. *" 'Forgive me, Father! I'm sorry!' Nuts! You don't have the guts of a real man. A man killed your son, and what do you do about it? Nothing! Not only are you yellow, but you're a liar. You hide your lack of manhood behind your 'goody-goody' Christianity. So be it; if you can't avenge your son, you can at least hate the man that killed him!"*

"I don't want to hate," I said. "How can I hate a man I've never seen? I hate what he did: getting drunk and running those two kids down—I hate that."

"Now that's a bunch of fake, pious, Christian hogwash if I ever heard it," he said. *"You don't hate the man, you hate the deed. Horse feathers! There's nothing wrong with hate—even God hates. Quit being a hypocrite. Hate him!"*

"No!" I cried. "Hate can destroy you. I've seen it happen to others. Leave me alone. I hate *you* for what you're trying to do."

"See, you can hate," he said. *"But why hate me? I didn't kill your son."*

"I'm not too sure you didn't," I replied. "You're probably behind all the drunkenness that goes on in the world. Liquor must be one of your most effective tools."

"Aw, come off it," Satan said. *"A little drink now and then never hurt anyone. Quit trying to change the subject. If you won't admit that you hate the man, then love him."*

"Boy! I walked into that one, didn't I?" I said. " 'Love him?' No way! I can't forgive him, either. Call me a hypocrite or a fake, if you like, but one thing I'm sure of: If that man had not been drunk, he wouldn't have killed those kids! You might as well place a gun in a drunk's hands as a high-powered auto."

"Get off your soapbox," he said. *"No one wants to hear a sermon on alcohol. Just because you don't like the 'sauce,' doesn't give you the right to force your hang-ups on others."*

"I'm not talking about drinking," I said, "even though you know better than anyone, the number of lives that have been destroyed by alcohol, I'd like to see your records. . . .

"No," I continued, "I've had too many acquaintences turn me off when I've brought up the subject of alcohol and its effects. People who drink don't seem to want to discuss the subject. I'm talking about drunk drivers. When someone tries to drown his miseries or conscience in booze, and does it at home, he only hurts himself and his loved ones. But when he gets in a car, that's an entirely different matter. But, why am I wasting my time arguing with you? There must be some other way. . . ."

I have not yet found that way. Every day I read in the newspaper of a continuing string of D.W.I. cases, tried, convicted and punished by small fines or probated sentences; and many of them are *second* and *third* offenses. The really frightening thing, however, is that the offenders continue to drive!

How can anyone be safe from drunk drivers? I don't see how friendly driving can protect you, or careful driving, or safer cars, or bicycle ordinances, or reflective clothing, or pedestrian crossings, or speed limits—or anything else!

Is there *nothing* we can do to keep drunks from behind the wheel?

It took sixteen months to bring the man who killed Ivy and Jody to trial. The district attorney's office estimates that it will take an additional eleven months before his appeal is heard. In the interval, I understand that there is no provision, in our state statutes, for suspension of the defendant's driving privileges. He has continued to drive, even though a jury found him guilty of murder without malice, and sentenced him to the maximum term of five years in the penitentiary.

I can't do anything for Jody now, he is with God; and his mother and I are free from the fear of nighttime sirens.

I know, however, that Ivy and Jody would want me to do what I can to keep this tragedy from happening to others.

I could remind you that this can happen to someone you love, or to you. But it probably would not register; it did not with me before that horrible night. I still have moments when my mind refuses to accept the fact that Jody is gone. There is a great aching void because I loved him as much as a father ever loved his son.

Though I grieve for Jody and Ivy, I grieve, also, for what seems to me to be a general indifference to the problem; for the fact that we may have, finally, arrived at the point where we accept, condone, excuse, laugh at, and thereby, actually *encourage* drunk driving.

Because my Lord loves me—selfish, weak, and sinful though I am; and because he has forgiven my sins, I should do no less than to forgive the man who killed my son. So far, it has not been possible, though I have prayed almost daily for help. Perhaps, someday, it will come.

I know this man did not wish to harm Ivy and Jody, and I pray, also, for him. It is not easy. But for me, there can be no other way.

11.
OBSERVATIONS ON GRIEF

Grief seems to be like the wind. Most of the time it surrounds us with gentle breezes, always present, but creating no conscious awareness.

Then, suddenly, we lose an acquaintance—one who is no more than a casual friend, and the breezes increase into moderate gusts that soon die down.

When we lose a close friend or a relative, outside our immediate family, the gusts become ominous gales that buffet us, pound us, and toss us about on angry seas.

Ultimately, we lose one who is among those most dear to us in all the world: a husband, a wife, a child, and those same winds which once blew so gently across our bodies, become the most awesome forces of violence and destruction imaginable. Like howling hurricanes, they threaten to rip us apart with their wild fury.

I have experienced the gentle breezes, the gusts, the gales, and the hurricanes of grief and, yet, there is so much that I still do not understand.

I look at a severely retarded child and wonder whether some afflictions are not worse than death; and then I look into the child's gentle eyes. I see the crooked, twisted smile, and I know how precious life is.

I remember a crippled, boyhood friend, his legs shriveled and useless, his body sagging in his crutches as he watched the other boys run and play. Instinctively, he reached into his pocket and withdrew a knife and a half-carved wooden horse. As he began to carve, I noticed the exquisite detail of the finished portion; and, even as a young boy, I understood the compensating gifts of God.

My older brother's wife is suffering from brain damage, and has been in a coma for over sixteen months. The last time I looked at her, I wondered if she could see, hear, understand. A lump rose in my throat, and I thought, "Does God have no mercy?" As I hurried out of the room, the question kept repeating itself over and over in my mind, and suddenly my question became another question, "Do you have no faith?" And, I had no answer.

Several years ago, Betsy's eighty-year-old, great-aunt was returning with us from my father-in-law's funeral. Suddenly she asked, "Why does God let me live so long? I'm a burden and of no use to anyone."

Out of sympathy, I said, "Now, Aunt Hattie, that's not true."

She replied, "Well now, just tell me, who am I any use to?"

I gulped a couple of times and wished I hadn't commented.

She chuckled at my embarrassment and added, "That's what I mean. Why does God let a useless, worn-out, old woman like me live on and on, and allow Betsy's dad to die when he had so much to live for?"

I had no answer for her, either. On and on, the questions parade before my mind even though, as I have said previously, I know there are no answers.

I am conscious of the fact that there are circumstances, other than death, which can cause grief: the breakup of a marriage, the misery of loneliness, the frustrations of defeat, the pain of illness, the torture of inadequacy. Suffering seems to know no bounds, and visits itself on the rich, the poor, the scholar, the illiterate, the strong, the weak, the male, and the female. It is the curse of mankind that, if a man lives, he will surely die; and if his years are long enough, he will surely know grief.

I must have, instinctively, known this before Jody was killed; because, without even being aware of it, I built myself a fortress, with moats and high walls and look-out towers and alarm systems. And I took my family inside with me, locked the door, and hung out a large "NO TRESPASSING" sign.

My fortress isolated me from the troubles, cares, and pains of those around me; from the fears I had of life; and even from God. I didn't know it at the time, but he walks among the poor, the lonely, the suffering, the dying—among miserable humanity everywhere.

Did he allow Jody to die to teach me a lesson—to show me the selfishness and isolation in my life? I don't know. For some reason, I prefer not to think so. I prefer to think Jody's death was simply a tragedy of life. But, through that tragedy, I am learning to become more sensitive to those around me.

Sitting alone in the assembly room of our church Bible class recently, my eyes came to rest on a portrait of Christ. The eyes fascinated me. I was drawn toward the portrait, and stood very close. As I looked into his eyes, I noticed a strange thing. The glass covering the portrait reflected the light in such way it acted like a dim mirror. My own face was superimposed over my Savior's face, and his eyes seemed to shine through mine.

I stood there *transfixed;* and the thought came to me, "O Lord, if only it could be like this, and I could so reflect your love!"

I have often wondered about the infinite love and compassion that our Savior's eyes must have held. He instantly drew all kinds of people to himself: from the simple fisherman, Peter, to the hated publican, Matthew. What magic did he have?

Some might call it charisma; but it was more than that. People don't give their lives for charmers, and many of his disciples gave their lives for his sake. Perhaps there was more in his eyes than compassion and love. Perhaps there was *pain*. The pain that came from bearing the sins of all humanity, from caring so much that he took unto himself the suffering of those to whom he ministered.

It is this Christ that is changing my life. He lives, more and more, in my *heart*, and my heart has begun to listen more carefully, speak more gently, and respond more sensitively. Let me share some recent examples:

A young woman of another faith knocked at my home recently, and asked if she could come in and discuss her church magazine with me. I said, "No, but you may come in and tell me about your pilgrimage with our Lord."

She agreed, and after she was seated, began to tell me about her church. I interrupted, and reminded her that I preferred to hear about her *personal* relationship with Christ. I said, "I don't want to offend you, but Christ has become so alive to me recently, that I'm interested in talking about him with others who know and love him."

She thought for a moment about what I had said and a smile came to her face as she replied: "I really want to tell you about my Lord, but I get my priorities mixed up. Yes, I'd like to tell you how Jesus has changed my life."

As I listened, I shook my head in wonder that one so

young could have known such loneliness and despair. But through the tears, her eyes brightened as she told me about meeting Jesus. It was a wonderful, heartwarming love story, and I thought back to the times I had, almost rudely, turned away others who had come as she had.

Our office receptionist buzzed me a few days ago to tell me that a man, whose name I did not know, wanted to see me on a personal matter. I asked her to invite him to my office.

As we sat down to talk, he said, "I'm not qualified to do anything, really, but I believe I could handle any job you've got. What kind'a work do you have?"

I asked what made him think we were looking for someone.

He said, "A fellow I know told me you were a successful businessman, and I decided I'd come see you."

"But you told the receptionist it was a personal matter," I replied.

"Yeah, I know," he said. "I wanted to talk to you, so, I just said it was a personal matter."

I started to usher him out, but there was something about him—as though he were trying to be bold, but inside he was scared. I sat back and said, "Well, since you asked to see me concerning a personal matter, why don't you tell me about it. What is it that frightens you?"

He sat silently for several moments and said, "How could you tell?"

"By looking into your eyes," I replied.

"Does it show that much?" he asked.

"Only to those who care," I said.

"Why do you care?" he asked. "You don't know me."

"It's hard to put into words," I said. "But Christ is changing my life, and people have become more important to me. I know what fear is and that makes it easier for me to recognize it in others."

He told me how circumstances had batted him around; how he could not hold a job, or support his family the way he wanted; how he was frustrated, and had begun to lose confidence in himself.

We talked about his feelings toward God and Christ, and I shared some of my experiences with him. I suggested he pray that the Christ he had known as a boy become real to him again; that he turn his fears and problems over to his Lord, and trust him.

As he stood up to leave, there were tears in his eyes. He took my hand in both of his and said, "Mr. Peerman, I've been thinking; when I said I wanted to see you about a personal matter, do you suppose God had anything to do with it?"

I nodded my head and added, "I think so, because I sensed the same feeling. Isn't it wonderful to know he loves us and cares for us?"

"Yes," he replied, "it is wonderful. It is also wonderful to know that someone like you cares. Thank you." As he walked out the door, there was music in my heart and I said, "Thank *you* Lord."

Ours is a secular world, a world in which it seems that many people believe in God, but few can freely and honestly talk about their relationship with him. There is a general acknowledgment of the existance of God. You hear it in expressions like: "God knows I'm telling the truth; Lord help me; Thank the good Lord; Oh, my God!" and others. But such phrases in our everyday speech bear out the point I'm trying to make. God is too often a fixture; the Bible, a dust-covered book on the shelf; and Christ, a plastic statue hanging from the rear-view mirror of a car.

That sounds cynical and I don't mean for it to be, but it bothers me. I'm not a preacher, or a theologian, or a Bible scholar, but every day God becomes more real to me, and I *must* share his love.

I feel some of the excitement of that small band of men in ancient Judea who walked the hot, dusty roads beside the man, Jesus of Nazareth. Men who watched in amazement as he performed miracles beyond their comprehension . . . who hung on his every word with little or no real understanding of the truths he spoke, knowing only that they could not live without him . . . who suffered in humiliation as he bathed their filthy feet . . . who stumbled along, helplessly, among the crowds, or maybe watched from afar, as he bore his cross to Golgotha and was crucified . . . whose very souls cried out in agony as they watched him die, knowing that it was finished, and they would never see him again.

But they *did* see him again. He had conquered death because he was more than man. He was God! And, in his victory, immortality was won for all men who believe.

CONCLUSION

This is my story, as I've stumbled from the dark valleys of grief, up the gentle hillsides and steep cliffs, through the scattered clouds, and toward the brilliant sunshine of the towering peaks. Among those peaks, my heavenly Father dwells. I cannot stay there for long, but someday I shall abide there forever.

Whatever conclusions I'm able to draw from life today may not necessarily be the same conclusions I'll draw tomorrow; for life isn't static, but is ever changing, and I must constantly change with it, if it is to be as full and rich as God intended.

But God is eternal and never changes, the same yesterday, today, and tomorrow. He is truth and the basis for all knowledge. He is also love and the basis for all human compassion.

I cannot understand the divine mysteries of life or death. Like Paul, I too, can only see through the glass dimly; but from what I can see, each of us is largely responsible for our own happiness and peace of mind.

Believing that God is love, I have concluded that there cannot be genuine happiness in my life without God for that would be a life without love. Love opens my heart to trust, to compassion, to sharing. Love sees only goodness and beauty; is patient and understanding and gentle. For me, love is the key that unlocks the secret door to happiness, to peace, to wishes, to dreams, and to God.

Do you ever dream of happiness that sends the heart soaring? I sought it through possessions, prestige, wealth, family, physical attractions, creative effort, business. I did not find it there.

I found it, almost by accident, among the broken pieces of my heart. A tiny corner of it sparkled like the edge of an uncut diamond, and as I rubbed it in my hands, I could see the radiance within. Somehow I knew that I held a precious gem—the love of God.

I knew also that I had to share it. Every time I give it away, I receive a larger stone in return—larger and more beautiful. My treasure house is never empty, but it grows richer each passing day.

Since Jody's death, the love I sought from others has seemed to come to me more and more. So many friends warmly embrace me, and from within the depths of their eyes and words, I can feel their caring. It is wonderful; and I react with appreciation, love, and gratitude to God.

I realize that I was self-sufficient, and in many ways I still am, but I am gradually changing. I need God and friends and love, and I need them more abundantly. And in my need, I become more aware of the needs of others, and, in this too, I am changing. Life seems sweeter in so many ways, and I hold almost tenaciously, to precious moments with loved ones, to the beauties that surround me, to the laughter of friends, and to quiet moments with God.

Four days ago I became the grandfather of a husky, healthy boy, Curtis Kelson Dyer, Jr., nicknamed "Kirk"—the son of our beloved Patti and Kelly. I am not yet accustomed to being a grandpa. My friends tell me there is nothing like it, and I believe them! I wonder what adorable name I will end up with: Paw-paw, Gang-ga, Pa, Grampie, Poppy? No matter, it is a wonderful, exciting experience, and I thank God for it.

What a miracle life is. When we first saw Kirk, he was screaming his little head off; obviously not too happy about being born, and why should he have been? In his mother's womb, his environment suited him fine: plenty of nourishment, warmth, peace, quiet, and genuine contentment.

And suddenly, he was jerked into a cold, noisy, blinding world; tugged at, turned this way and that, rubbed, scrubbed, and slapped on the back. No wonder he was screaming. Later, he would learn how good life could be, but not then. Given his choice, I suspect he would have preferred putting birth off for a while.

Most of us seem to come into life that way; perhaps it's the same when we die: *We would just as soon put it off for a while.* After birth, we soon discover mother in all her tenderness, and we begin to know love. Then life becomes sweet and exciting and wonderful. After death, we will discover God in all his glory and then we'll know *ultimate love* beyond our wildest imagination. This is the glorious promise of the Christian faith.

And so life goes on. There is a right time for everything: a time to be born, a time to die, a time to cry, a time to laugh, a time to grieve, a time to dance, a time to lose, and a time to find. . . .

Blindly, I stumble on in my Christian pilgrimage, taking each day's journey as God unfolds it; seeking to know his will, and praising him for the salvation of his love.

I know I shall continue to miss Jody for the remainder of my days. I loved him so very much, and I still grieve over his tragic, senseless death. His image flashes before my mind's eye so many times during my waking hours, and he frequently appears in my dreams; but God's miracle of time spins its magic and little by little, the grief is becoming bearable. Through the tears that well into my eyes, I can see him even now: his laughing, happy face, his youthful exuberance, his gentle compassion. I can see him so clearly; he seems to be saying, "Good-night, Dad."

"Good-night, Buddy, I love you. *'See you in the morning.'* "

WITHDRAWN

Date Due